the dad who didn't know

to all who wriggle

Illustrations by Adam Carnegie

Published by
Conscious Stories LLC
1831 12th Ave South, Suite 118
Nashville, TN 37203

www.consciousstories.com

First Edition
Library of Congress
Control Number: 2017901955
ISBN 978-1-943750-04-7

The last 20 minutes of every day are precious.

Dear parents, teachers, and readers,

This story has been gift-wrapped with two simple mindfulness practices to help you connect more deeply with your children in the last 20 minutes of each day.

● Quietly set your intention for calm, open connection.

● Then start your story time with the **Snuggle Breathing Meditation**. Read each line aloud and take slow, deep breaths together in order to relax and be present.

● At the end of the story, you can **Sail The Seas Of Knowledge**. There are four simple questions to help your children feel okay about not knowing everything.

Enjoy snuggling into togetherness!

Andrew

Snuggle Breathing

Our story begins with us breathing together.
Say each line aloud and then
take a slow deep breath in and out.

I breathe for me

I breathe for you

I breathe for us

I breathe for all that surrounds us

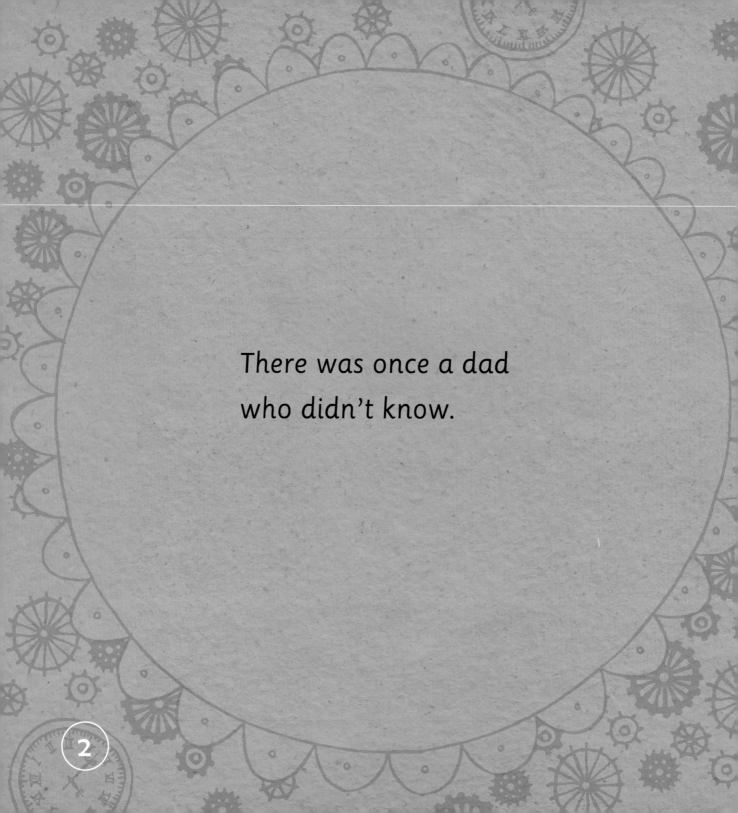

There was once a dad
who didn't know.

This book ~~belongs to:~~
is shared with

_____

_____

_____

He had two
delightful children
and a beautiful wife
whom he dearly loved.

Each morning he went to work
wearing a smart suit and driving a smart car.
He worked hard all day and looked forward
to coming home to his loving family.

This dad lived in two worlds.

His **Outside World**
and his **Inside World**.
Both were very busy!

On the **outside** he was busy with
work, house repairs, and computer-y things.

On the **inside** he dreamt of
sunny days and fun with
his family.

6

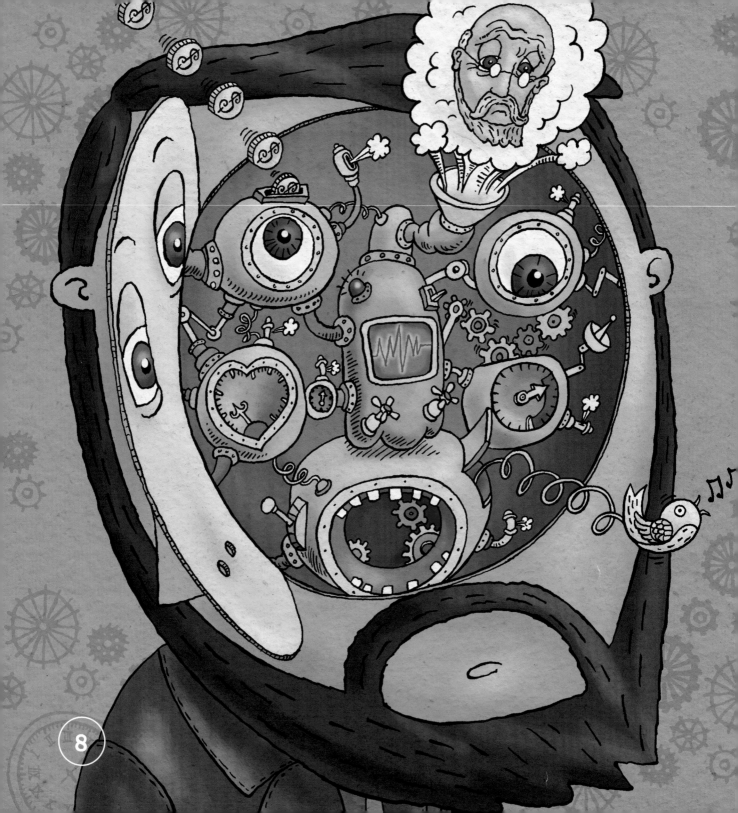

On the inside he also worried a lot.

He worried about money.
He worried about getting old.
He worried that his family
didn't know he loved them.

His son asked him to play catch,
but he felt too tired.
His daughter wanted to bounce
on his knee, but he had a sore back.
His wife wanted to plan a family holiday,
but he worried about money.

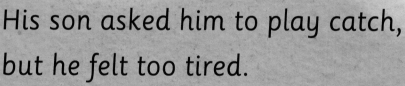

This dad wanted to do these wonderful things, but something always got in the way.

He didn't know how
to find his smile when he was sad.
He didn't know how
to ask for help when he was tired.
He didn't know how
to make his dreams come true.

13

"I'm **the dad**. I'm supposed to know," he thought.

But he didn't know,
so he wriggled and squirmed
to get away from the
yucky feeling in his belly.

Over time his **Inside World**
became very lonely.

He forgot about the joy of sunny days.
He forgot about his happy dreams.
He even forgot about fun with his family

Luckily, the story doesn't end here.

His daughter knew where to find her smile when she was sad. She would dance and sing.

His wife knew where to find help when she was tired. She would pray and read.

His son knew how to make his dreams come true. He patiently watched nature do it every day.

Their dancing, prayers, and patience
surrounded this dad with love.

23

Like magic,
a little light sparked deep **inside**.

For one moment he stopped
wriggling and squirming.

He took a deep breath…
sighed…
and sat down.

Phew!

He looked around, smiling.

"I feel relaxed and happy
on the **inside** and the **outside**!"

"I don't even know how that happened!"

"But I am the dad, and I **should** know," he thought, almost wriggling and squirming again.

Just then,
his daughter danced past,
his son picked a flower, and
his wife turned a page.

"Aha!" he smiled.
"They know how to be happy!
I will learn from them."

"I am the dad, and
**I don't need to know
...everything!**"

Andrew Newman – author

Andrew Newman is the award-winning author and founder of www.ConsciousStories.com, a growing series of bedtime stories purpose-built to support parent-child connection in the last 20 minutes of the day. His professional background includes deep training in therapeutic healing work and mindfulness. He brings a calm yet playful energy to speaking events and workshops, inviting and encouraging the creativity of his audiences, children K-5, parents, and teachers alike.

Adam Carnegie - illustrator

Adam is a specialist children's book illustrator with 23 years of experience. He lives in Cape Town, South Africa with his wife and family. He is a passionate educator and environmentalist with a deep love of the outdoors, especially surfing. Adam writes, "While almost all my work is digital, I still do all my draft works in pencil and, usually, my finished art line with dipped pen and ink."

www.behance.net/Adamada

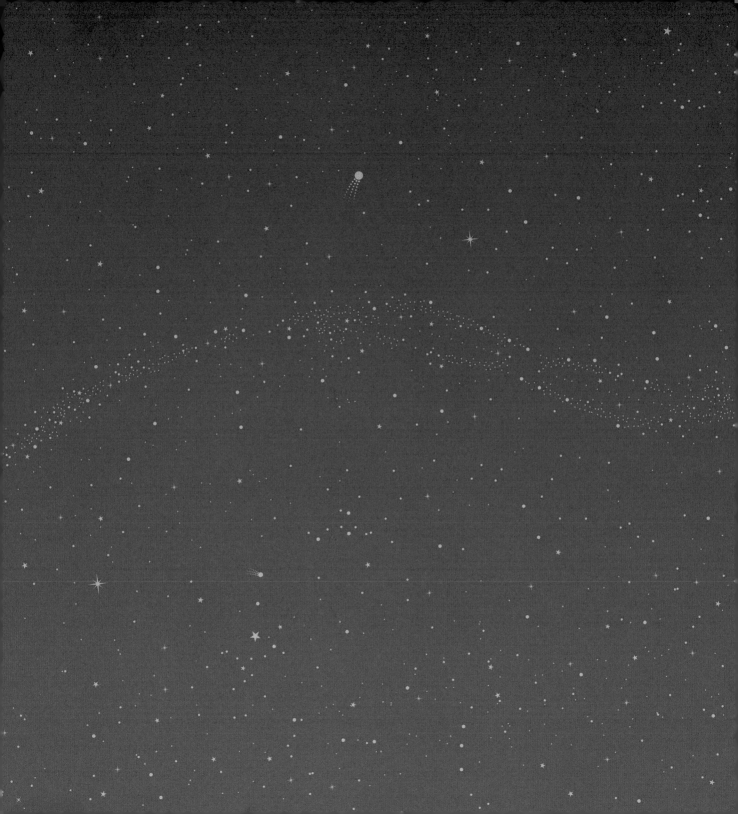

Star Counter

Every time you breathe together and read aloud, you make a star shine in the night sky.

Color in a star to count how many times you have read this book.